Freedom

Wendy Macdonald
Illustrated by Warren Crossett

A Harcourt Achieve Imprint

www.Rigby.com
1-800-531-5015

Literacy by Design Leveled Readers: *Freedom*

ISBN-13: 978-1-4189-3663-1
ISBN-10: 1-4189-3663-4

Printed in China
3 4 5 6 7 8 985 14 13 12 11 10 09 08

Contents

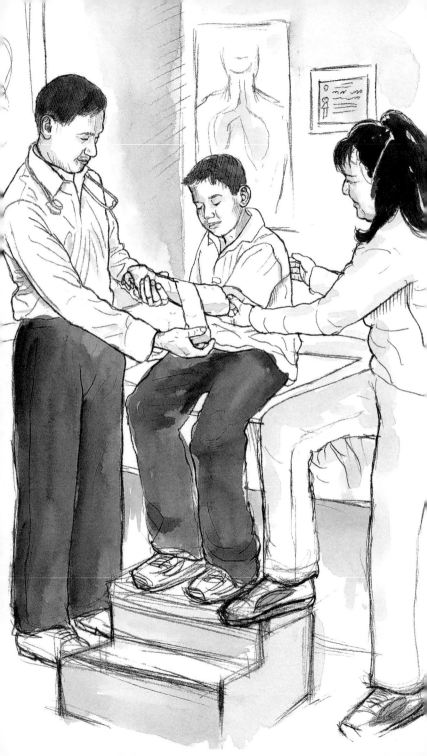

Chapter 1

Diego Sees
an Eagle

Diego Garza's arm ached, and the cast on it was stiff and heavy.

"It will be sore for a few days, then we'll take a look at it in about six weeks," said the doctor, cheerfully. Diego did not look happy.

"Six weeks!" he thought. "Nearly my whole vacation will be ruined because of this cast that makes it feel like I'm carrying a brick around."

"Come on, Diego," said Mom with a smile on her face, trying to cheer him up. "Let's go home." And she led Diego out of the doctor's office.

It began the day before when Diego was playing with his tennis racket and ball. He hit a beautiful shot, but the ball got stuck in the roof's gutter. Diego climbed up the fence and onto the roof. He found the ball and threw it down. Then he thought he could swing himself down from the gutter because he didn't think it was too far to fall.

But the gutter gave way and dropped him onto the ground. Without thinking, he put out a hand to break his fall. Suddenly, he felt a sharp pain run up his arm and knew at that moment that his arm was broken.

When they got home from the doctor's office, his mother wheeled his bike inside the garage.

"I don't think you should ride your bike for awhile, Diego," she said.

"Can't do this. Can't do that," grumbled Diego. "It's like I'm in jail."

Diego wandered into the field behind his family's ranch and sat down with his back against the fence. He watched a bird high up in the sky. The bird had big wings, but they hardly seemed to move. It rose higher and higher in the air, when suddenly it folded its wings against its body and dived. Then it fluttered its wings, rolled, and drifted up again. It rose and rose until it was only a tiny dot in the sky and Diego could not see it anymore.

That night, he told his father about the bird, "It went so high that I couldn't see it," he said.

"That's old Sharp-Eye, the eagle," said Dad, "and I think it lives on top of Mount Beacon."

Mount Beacon was a steep, rocky peak that was on the Garza's land.

"You might have lost sight of the bird," Dad went on, "but it probably could see you. Eagles have very sharp eyes, and they can see little animals like mice and rabbits moving on the ground—that's how they live. They swoop down and pick them up. Next time you go out, take my binoculars so you'll be able to see it then."

Chapter 2

Skyrider

Every day after that, Diego watched for the eagle, which did live on top of Mount Beacon.

"How does it fly?" he asked his father. "It doesn't seem to move its wings."

"An eagle is the best flier in the world," Dad said. "It glides on warm air currents, and it can do stunts that make pilots look inexperienced."

Diego admired the bird's grace and beauty even more now. His father called it Sharp-Eye, but Diego called the eagle Skyrider.

One day he saw another bird appear in the sky. It was smaller and darker than Skyrider, but as it soared over Mount Beacon, the eagle turned and flew angrily toward it. The smaller bird swung upward and flew off. The eagle didn't chase it and continued to float peacefully through the air, but the second bird didn't disappear. It dived at the eagle. This time, Skyrider turned to meet it with its talons outstretched.

When he told Dad what he had seen, his dad said, "Maybe the other bird was a hawk or a falcon. Eagles like to have their space to themselves. They don't like to share."

Chapter 3
Mid-Air Battle

The next day, Diego was sitting in the field watching Skyrider. It was hunting when it must have seen something, for it began to glide downward in wide circles.

Suddenly, from above the eagle, another bird dived down. It seemed to appear out of nowhere, but Skyrider had heard it, and with a flick of its wings rolled to face the other bird.

The second bird dived at the eagle. Again, Skyrider rolled and this time struck at the other bird with its sharp claws. This was too much for the smaller bird so it pulled quickly out of its dive, flying away just above Skyrider's wings and narrowly avoiding a crash. Then it rose steeply and hurried off into the distance.

But the eagle had already been nearing the ground when the smaller bird struck. Before it could rise to safety, Skyrider crashed into the trees.

"Oh, no!" gasped Diego. "Skyrider's down." He began to run toward the place where the bird had disappeared near the foot of Mount Beacon.

There, beneath a big tree, in a pile of sticks and leaves, was Skyrider with blood on one wing and the other wing trailing uselessly on the ground. Diego ran to get help.

Chapter 4

Skyrider Is Down

"Dad!" he shouted, bursting into the house. "Skyrider is down, it's lying on the ground, and it can't fly."

"Slow down," said Dad calmly. "Who is Skyrider?"

"It's the eagle I was talking about!"

"OK, we'll call Dr. Harding to see what she says." (Dr. Harding was the local vet.)

After he had made the phone call, Dad said to Diego, "Now show me where it is."

Skyrider was flapping its good wing on the ground, and flies were already buzzing around the wounded one.

"You need to stay away, Diego," said Dad. "One slash from those claws and you'll be in trouble."

It wasn't long before Dr. Harding drove up and took a blanket out of her car. "I'm going to throw this blanket over it so it can't see," she said.

Dr. Harding dropped the blanket over the eagle and tied the bird's legs with a piece of rope. Soon the bird was bundled up in the doctor's car and was being driven into town.

Chapter 5
Diego Is Worried

Later that week, Diego and his dad went into town to see the wounded bird. Diego's arm was much stronger now, and he hardly noticed the cast. But there was one thing that worried him. What would happen to Skyrider when its wing was better? Diego decided to ask Dr. Harding.

"The city zoo," said Dr. Harding, "is very anxious to have such a fine bird, but don't worry," she added, "Skyrider will be well taken care of at the zoo. It will probably live a lot longer there than it would in the wild."

But Diego knew that there were no mice or squirrels at the zoo to catch Skyrider's sharp eyes, and no currents of warm air for it to play on. Nobody there would ever know what a terrific flier it was, and in time, Skyrider might forget, too.

That night, Diego couldn't stop thinking about Skyrider and the cage it would be in. Somehow the two just didn't fit. What could he do? At last he thought of something, so he set his alarm and went to sleep.

Just before sunrise, the alarm went off, and Diego switched it off quickly before anyone else would hear it. After he got dressed, he took his bike and went into town.

The road was quiet and empty. He was pedaling up the main street before the first truck passed him, but then his heart sank, for he recognized that truck. It belonged to Joe Ridley, who owned the local pick-up and delivery service, and it was stopping right in front of Dr. Harding's house. Diego knew Joe was there to pick up Skyrider. Once the cage was on the truck, Skyrider would be gone for good.

Chapter 6

A Race Against Time

When Diego reached Dr. Harding's house, Joe Ridley was standing at the door, and Diego could hear Dr. Harding's voice. "Wait here, Joe," she was saying, "and I'll get my keys."

In a few minutes, Joe would come back to the truck and drive it down the lane to the field where Skyrider was. He would pick up Skyrider's cage and take off for the zoo. There was absolutely no time to lose. Diego had to move quickly!

When Diego got to the field, he pulled the bolt back and the cage door swung open by itself. "Come on," whispered Diego. "The door's open, so off you go."

Skyrider didn't move. Diego heard the truck door slam and the sound of the engine starting. "Do you want to be stuck in a cage for your whole life?"

Then he heard the truck's engine cough and die.

In the still air, Diego could hear Dr. Harding's voice. "What's wrong, Joe?"

Joe answered her, but all Diego could hear was mumbling. There was a rattle as the hood of the truck was thrown open.

Diego looked around him and saw a branch lying on the ground nearby. He poked it through the wire and pushed it gently against Skyrider's side, encouraging the bird toward the door. He heard the truck hood slam shut, and the engine started again. This time, it settled into a steady rumble.

"Hurry up," Diego groaned, "they'll be here in a minute. If you don't go now, it will be too late."

Skyrider gave a little hop, its wings began to beat, and with a *whoosh*, the bird was airborne. Joe's truck bounced down the lane and stopped at the gate just as Skyrider was rising into the bright sky.

Diego set off for home as fast as he could, keeping away from the roads that he thought Joe might use.

29

Chapter 7

Freedom

At lunch that day, Dad said,
"Joe Ridley told me he drove into town
this morning to take your eagle to the
zoo, Diego, but the cage must have
come open somehow, because the bird
was gone."

"That's good," said Diego. "Now it
can be free."

"Hmm ..." said Dad, as he bent
forward and plucked a small twig from
Diego's hair. It was a tiny flower from
Dr. Harding's bushes.

"Now you can be free, too," said Mom. "Have you forgotten that today is the day your cast comes off?"

That afternoon they drove to the city, and the doctor cut the cast off Diego's arm. When it was gone, his arm felt light and strange.

That evening, Diego went out into the field and saw a black speck way up high. Skyrider was circling Mount Beacon. Diego waved his arm at the wonderful bird.

Was it his imagination, or did the wide wings wave in reply? "Freedom," he thought. "There's nothing like it."